A Practical Guide to
RIDING & PONY CARE

Christopher Rawson, Joanna Spector and Elizabeth Polling

Consultant and contributor: Patricia Smyly

Illustrated by Eric Rowe and Fred'k. St. Ward
Designed by Bob Scott

Contents

USBORNE

Getting to Know a Pony

Learning to ride is great fun but there is much more to it than just sitting in a saddle. If you find out about horses and ponies and how to handle them, you will learn to ride well and happily.

Ponies are gentle but strong and should be handled quietly and firmly. They are startled by sudden noises and movements, so talk to a pony before you go up to him or touch him. Then he will get to know your voice and trust you.

1 Catching a Pony

Go into the field, taking his headcollar and a titbit, such as a sliced carrot. Remember to close the gate behind you. If a pony lives on his own, give him a call.

2

If he is with others, keep the titbit in your pocket and walk to him, talking quietly. Offer the carrot from your left hand as you slip the lead rope over his head.

Measuring a Pony

Height is measured in hands from the ground to the top of your pony's withers. One hand equals 4 ins or about 10 cms. Take off one centimetre for his shoes.

Points of a Horse

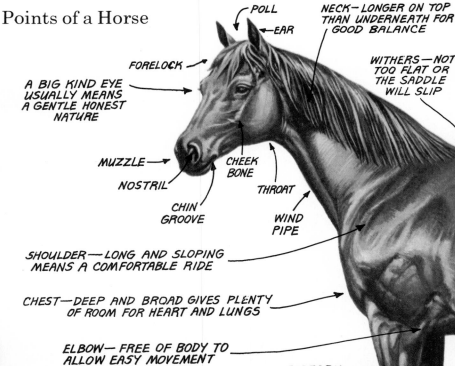

POLL

EAR

NECK—LONGER ON TOP THAN UNDERNEATH FOR GOOD BALANCE

FORELOCK

A BIG KIND EYE USUALLY MEANS A GENTLE HONEST NATURE

WITHERS—NOT TOO FLAT OR THE SADDLE WILL SLIP

MUZZLE

NOSTRIL

CHEEK BONE

CHIN GROOVE

THROAT

WIND PIPE

SHOULDER—LONG AND SLOPING MEANS A COMFORTABLE RIDE

CHEST—DEEP AND BROAD GIVES PLENTY OF ROOM FOR HEART AND LUNGS

ELBOW—FREE OF BODY TO ALLOW EASY MOVEMENT

RIBS

FOREARM

OFF FORE LEG

KNEE

NEAR FORE LEG

A SHORT CANNON BONE IS STRONG

FETLOCK

ER

CORONET BAND

HOOV HARD A STRON

Face Markings

Star

Snip

Blaze

Stripe

Leg Markings

Sock

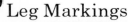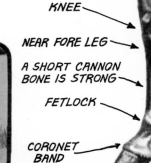
Stocking

3 While he is munching, put on the headcollar. Give him a pat and another titbit to reward him for being caught or he may not want to come to you next time.

4 Take the rope like this. Say "Walk on" and move forward. You should be able to walk at a pony's shoulder. Practise leading him from both sides.

5 Never do this. Most ponies dislike being stared in the face and pull back. You can teach a pony to walk forward by tapping his side gently with a stick as you move.

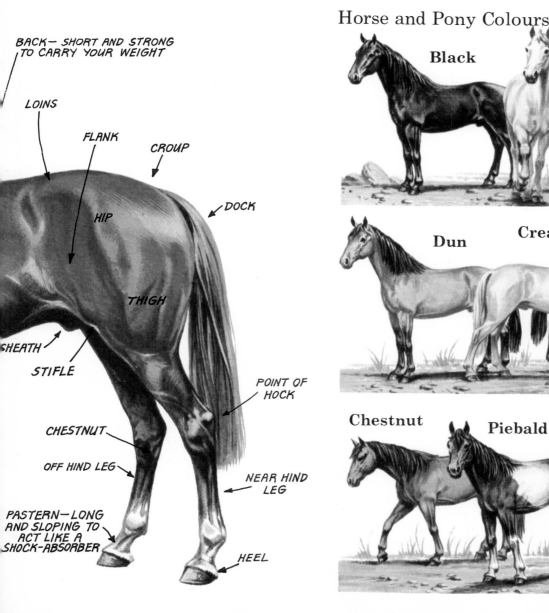

BACK— SHORT AND STRONG TO CARRY YOUR WEIGHT

LOINS

FLANK

CROUP

DOCK

HIP

THIGH

SHEATH

STIFLE

POINT OF HOCK

CHESTNUT

OFF HIND LEG

NEAR HIND LEG

PASTERN— LONG AND SLOPING TO ACT LIKE A SHOCK-ABSORBER

HEEL

Horse and Pony Colours

Black

Grey

Bay

Dun

Cream

Roan

Chestnut

Piebald

Skewbald

Saddles and Bridles

Saddles and bridles and other pieces of pony equipment are called tack. Tacks cost a lot but if you look after it well it will last for many years. Always try on new or secondhand tack if you are buying, as a pony will never be happy if it does not fit.

A saddle should fit without touching a pony's spine when your weight is on it. But check that it is not so high that the saddle is perched on his back. If it is, it will roll about and unbalance you both. It should not be too tight over his withers, nor too long over his loins. A general-purpose saddle you can use for riding and jumping, and a snaffle bridle, are probably the best to choose.

Keep the saddle on a bracket or saddle horse, and the bridle hanging by the headpiece. Store them in a dry place when you are not using them. Never leave a pony untied wearing his saddle as he may roll on it and damage it.

Parts of the Saddle

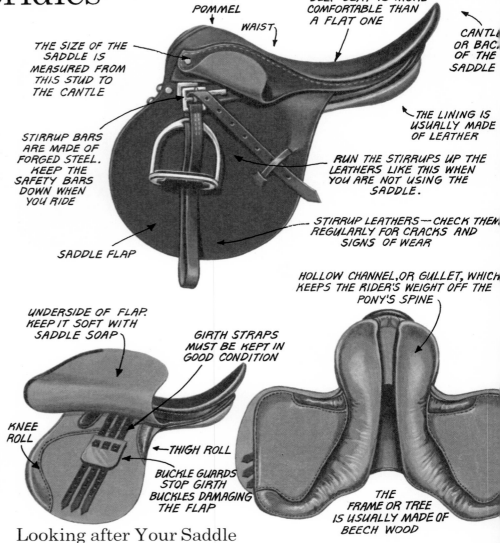

POMMEL

WAIST

SEAT—A SADDLE WITH A DEEP SEAT IS MORE COMFORTABLE THAN A FLAT ONE

CANTLE OR BACK OF THE SADDLE

THE SIZE OF THE SADDLE IS MEASURED FROM THIS STUD TO THE CANTLE

THE LINING IS USUALLY MADE OF LEATHER

STIRRUP BARS ARE MADE OF FORGED STEEL. KEEP THE SAFETY BARS DOWN WHEN YOU RIDE

RUN THE STIRRUPS UP THE LEATHERS LIKE THIS WHEN YOU ARE NOT USING THE SADDLE.

STIRRUP LEATHERS—CHECK THEM REGULARLY FOR CRACKS AND SIGNS OF WEAR

SADDLE FLAP

UNDERSIDE OF FLAP. KEEP IT SOFT WITH SADDLE SOAP

GIRTH STRAPS MUST BE KEPT IN GOOD CONDITION

KNEE ROLL

THIGH ROLL

BUCKLE GUARDS STOP GIRTH BUCKLES DAMAGING THE FLAP

HOLLOW CHANNEL, OR GULLET, WHICH KEEPS THE RIDER'S WEIGHT OFF THE PONY'S SPINE

THE FRAME OR TREE IS USUALLY MADE OF BEECH WOOD

Looking after Your Saddle

Clean your saddle after every ride. Take off the girth and stirrups. Damp-sponge off the dirt. Dry the leather, then rub in saddle soap. Polish the stirrups and clean the girth. Lastly, put everything back in place. If the saddle is new, it is a good idea to oil it to make it more supple. Every year have it checked by a saddler.

Saddling Up

1 Tie up your pony. Smooth the hair on his back, then put on the saddle, like this, from the nearside. Keep the front of the saddle well forward over his withers.

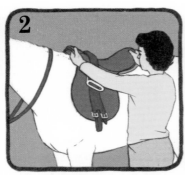

2 Slide it back into place. Go to the offside and let down the girth, checking that the flap and buckles are not caught or twisted. Return to the nearside and do up the girth.

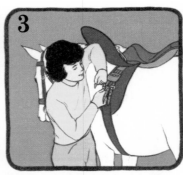

3 Tighten the girth gently, gradually smoothing the hair and skin under it. Some ponies puff themselves out, so check the girth again before and after you get on.

Removing a Saddle

Run the stirrups up the leathers. Undo the girth on the nearside, then lift off the saddle on to your left arm. Pick up the girth as it comes off and lay it across the saddle.

4

Girths

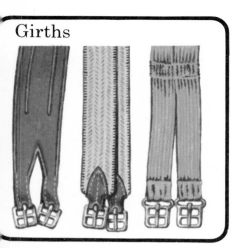

A girth is a belt which is buckled round your pony to keep the saddle in place. Good ones are made of nylon, string or leather which must be kept soft.

A Jumping Saddle

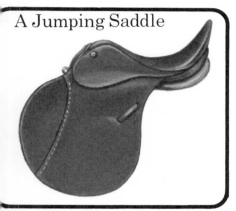

These usually have very light trees so they weigh as little as possible. They also have flaps shaped like this to help keep you in the right position for jumping.

Parts of a Bridle

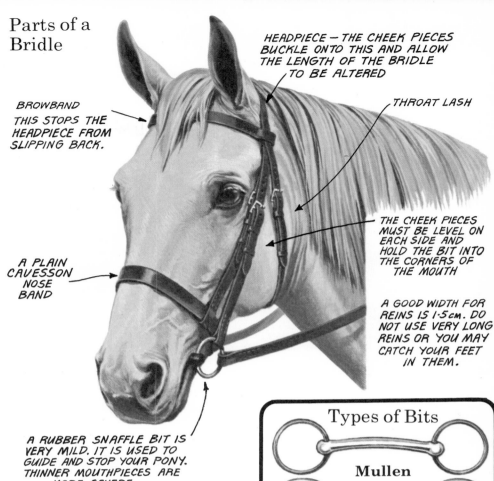

HEADPIECE — THE CHEEK PIECES BUCKLE ONTO THIS AND ALLOW THE LENGTH OF THE BRIDLE TO BE ALTERED

BROWBAND THIS STOPS THE HEADPIECE FROM SLIPPING BACK.

THROAT LASH

THE CHEEK PIECES MUST BE LEVEL ON EACH SIDE AND HOLD THE BIT INTO THE CORNERS OF THE MOUTH

A PLAIN CAVESSON NOSE BAND

A GOOD WIDTH FOR REINS IS 1·5cm. DO NOT USE VERY LONG REINS OR YOU MAY CATCH YOUR FEET IN THEM.

A RUBBER SNAFFLE BIT IS VERY MILD. IT IS USED TO GUIDE AND STOP YOUR PONY. THINNER MOUTHPIECES ARE MORE SEVERE

Looking after Your Bridle

Wash the bit after your ride so food and saliva do not dry on it. To clean the bridle, undo all the buckles and wipe each piece separately. Dry it with a chamois leather, then rub in saddle soap with an almost dry sponge. Put it together again ready to use.

Types of Bits

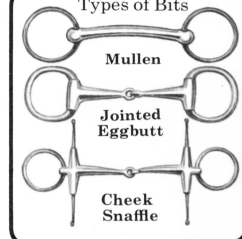

Mullen

Jointed Eggbutt

Cheek Snaffle

Fitting a Bridle

1

Slip the reins over his head, then, holding the bridle like this, open his mouth with your thumb. Gently push in the bit. At the same time, lift the headpiece over his ears.

2

Straighten his mane and lift his forelock over the browband. Check that the bit hangs level across the top of his tongue and up against his lips without wrinkling them.

3

Do up the noseband and throatlash. Your hand should fit under the throatlash, like this. Put all the straps neatly in their keepers so they will not flap about.

Removing a Bridle

Undo the noseband and throatlash. Lift the reins and headpiece gently over his ears, like this. Allow him to drop the bit from his mouth as you pull off the bridle.

A Pony of Your Own

Everyone who likes riding dreams of having their own pony. Choosing one is great fun, but takes a lot of time and has to be done carefully.

Before you buy a pony, get as much experience as you can. This will help you to know what you are looking for and choose the right one.

You also need to learn how to feed a pony, catch him in a field, groom him, and put on his saddle and bridle before yo look after your own.

1 What a Pony Needs

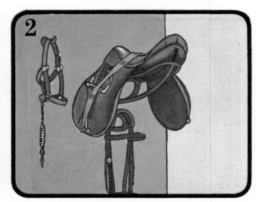

It is cheaper for you, and better for your pony, if he lives out in a field. There should be at least one acre of good grazing for each pony in the field.

2

The pony will need a saddle, bridle and a headcollar. Unless you take over the tack belonging to the pony you buy, ask your saddler to come and fit the new tack correctly.

3

In winter some ponies kept out at grass need a New Zealand rug. The also need extra food then. Find out if your local feed merchant can sell you hay and pony nuts.

4

5

Every four to six weeks, the blacksmith should take off your pony's shoes, trim his feet and replace the worn shoes with new ones. This takes about an hour.

6

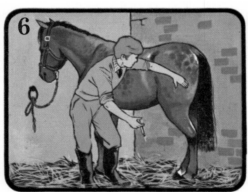

Your pony should be treated for worms every eight to ten weeks to keep him healthy. Once a year the vet should inject him against 'flu and tetanus and check his health.

7

Here are some of the things you w need for grooming your pony. It is a good idea to get them before you buy a pony. If you look after them they will last a very long time.

Choosing the Right Size

It is better to buy a pony that is a little too big for you at first. Then you can still ride him as you grow older. But he should not be so big you cannot control him. If your pony is too small, you will not be comfortable and he may not be able to carry you for long. If you want to ride in competitions, make sure your pony's height is not over the class limit.

Pony Too Big

Pony Too Small

What to Look For

The more you know about a pony before you buy it, the better. Look for one whose owner has outgrown it or one you already know, perhaps from a local riding school. Take someone with you who knows a lot about horses.

Do not buy at an auction as you cannot ride the ponies. Choose a pony that is between 6 and 14 years old and has been fully schooled. See him in a field. Is he friendly and easy to catch? Have him saddled and ridden. Then ride him.

If he seems to like being ridden and walks quietly in noisy traffic, ask a good horse vet to check that he is healthy. If all is well and you are sure this is the pony you want, then you can go ahead and buy him.

Enjoying a Pony

You will enjoy riding on an ordinary steady pony. You can also compete in many events at local gymkhanas and Pony Club rallies. Ponies usually enjoy hunting and jumping natural fences, such as

logs and ditches. Most can learn quite easily to jump a course of show jumps up to about one metre high. But highly-trained show jumpers are very expensive. They need courage to tackle big jumps

and so may be too excitable to be good first ponies. Showing classes are like beauty contests—ponies must look good and move well.

Keeping a Pony at Grass

Ponies are happier living with others, so try to share your field with a friend who has one too. Make sure they have food, water and shelter.

Your field should be fenced with post and rails, strong hedges or plain wire. Be careful with barbed wire as it can easily injure a pony. Wire should be pulled very tight with the bottom strand at least 46 cm high.

Ponies like to eat short juicy grass. They do not like the long coarse grass where droppings have fallen.

If you do not look after your field, it may become "horse sick". This means that the parts which ponies eat are bare, and other parts are covered in long, useless grass. Ponies get worms if they eat the eggs of worms which live in droppings. It is a good idea to clear up droppings regularly. It helps to let cows graze the field and eat the long grass.

A shelter like this, facing South, is ideal. But a thick hedge on the north side of a field is good enough shelter for most ponies.

The best water supply is trough which fills up automatically as your pony drinks. It should be cleaned out regularly.

Check your pony often for injuries. Pick out his feet. See that his shoes are in good order.

The gate must be strong and have a catch that ponies cannot undo. It is wise to have a chain and padlock as well.

1 Extra Feeding

Your pony will need hay when grass is scarce and has little goodness in it. This is usually from October to May. Putting it in a hay net hitched up high, like this, saves waste. He will need between 2½ and 5 kilos a day, depending on his size. Always feed hay which has a sweet smell. Mouldy hay could make your pony ill or damage his breathing.

2

Ponies that look well when fed on hay alone, may not need anything else. But if your pony is working hard he will need extra food, such as nuts. They are easy to use but expensive. Feed from about 1 kilo to a very small pony up to 3 kilos to a 14 hand pony, split into 2 small feeds. Read about other sorts of food on the next two pages.

Some ponies enjoy a salt or mineral lick. Put a block in a sheltered place for him.

This is a post-and-rail fence. It is the best for ponies as it is strong and they cannot injure themselves on it.

Never tie a pony to a fence, in case he is frightened and pulls it down.

Poisonous Plants

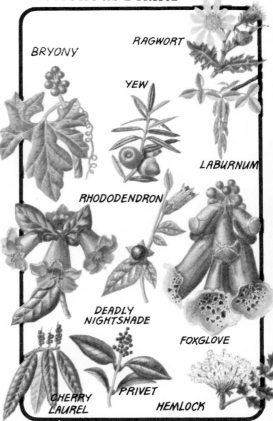

BRYONY

RAGWORT

YEW

LABURNUM

RHODODENDRON

DEADLY NIGHTSHADE

FOXGLOVE

CHERRY LAUREL

PRIVET

HEMLOCK

Search your field and hedges for poisonous plants before putting your pony in. Uproot any you find and burn them. Put a fence round any harmful shrubs or trees to keep them out of reach. Too many acorns are poisonous but most ponies do not eat them.

Grooming

Brush off dry mud with a dandy brush, but do not brush too much as this will remove the natural grease which keeps your pony dry and warm. Tidy his mane and tail, sponge his eyes, nose and dock and pick out his feet.

Cold Weather

Your pony can stay outside even in weather like this, as long as he has extra food to keep him warm. Give him at least as much as a stabled pony. When it freezes, do not forget to break the ice on his water trough every day.

A New Zealand Rug

This is a waterproof rug which your pony can wear during the winter, if he is part-clipped or if he does not grow a thick coat. Make sure it fits correctly and check it every day or it may begin to rub and make him sore.

Stables and Feeding

If you ride a lot and your pony needs to be really fit, it is best to keep him stabled. Clip his thick winter coat so he does not sweat and lose weight, and keep him warm with a rug.

There is no need to keep him in all the time. A few hours a day in the field will keep him happy and easy to manage. Try to stick to a regular routine, such as this, which suits you and your pony:
7.30 am—Give water, a feed, a small haynet and muck out.
10.00 am— Brush your pony, pick out his feet, exercise for at least an hour. 12.00—Small fee and turn out till tea time.
4.00 pm—Groom thoroughly, bed down. About 5.00 pm— Fill water bucket, and haynet, give evening feed. Before you g to bed check all is well.

The Stable

A loose box, like this, with a divided door is ideal. A strong shed can often be used. It should be at least 3 x 4 metres, with a high roof and a doorway 1.20 metres wide. Rough concrete, to stop him slipping, makes a good floor. It should slope down slightly towar the drain.

Feeding

Ponies have small stomachs for their size so they need to eat little and often. The basic food that replaces grass for stabled ponies is hay, which is a bulk food. They also need other sorts of food to give them energy. All ponies need different amounts.

Good hay should have a sweet smell, and be crisp to feel. Never feed musty or mouldy hay, nor hay that is less than six months old. Give less energy food if you cannot exercise your pony. Be sure he has water to drink before each feed.

Energy Foods

These are the most important part of a hard working pony's diet. They make him strong and fit and ready to work.

Barley

This is a good fattening food but not so heating as oats. Feed it well crushed or boil whole grains for 2-3 hours.

Oats

These can make ponies hot and excitable, so fee only small amounts, wel crushed, to begin with. They should be clean, an at least six months old.

Maize

This is not so full of protein as oats but shou still only be fed in very small quantities.

Looking after the Stable

Tools You Will Need

Cover the floor with deep bedding to keep your pony comfortable and warm. Wheat straw is best, except for a greedy pony who may eat it and get too fat or even ill. Peat, wood shavings, sawdust or shredded paper are also good.

Muck out each morning. Remove the droppings and wet straw. Stack the clean straw in a corner and brush the floor. Re-lay the bed, banking it round the walls. Add clean straw when it is needed, which may not be every day.

Buy good tools that you can handle easily. Use a basket or skep to carry droppings from the stable. You will also need a broom, a shovel and at least one fork. Do not use a fork with sharp prongs as this could be dangerous.

Rugging Up

A jute rug is usually put on a clipped pony at night, in winter, with one or two underblankets. In daytime, a woollen rug is useful inside, and a New Zealand rug for outside. Throw it on like this.

Make sure it is well forward. Then do up the front buckle. From the back, pull the rug into place. Walk round to the off side to make sure that the rug is hanging evenly and is not caught up.

Put on the roller and do it up tight enough to keep the rug in place. Smooth out any creases. To take off the rug, remove the roller, undo the front buckle and slide it off backwards.

Bulk Foods

These are parts of your pony's diet which help to fill him up. They also stop him eating the energy food too quickly.

Sugar Beet Pulp

This must be soaked for 24 hours before feeding.

Chaff

This is hay which has been put through a chaff cutter. This should be done little and often or chaff will become dusty.

Bran

Bran is a useful bulk food. It is the ground outer husks of wheat. It can be fed dry with oats or damp in a mash. Warm bran mash is good for sick ponies.

Nuts

There are lots of different sorts of pony nuts. Mostly they are a ready-made mixture of energy and bulk food which gives your pony the same balanced diet all the time. There are other sorts, called low-protein nuts which are mainly dried grass. They are all easy to store and feed. Some fresh greenery or vegetables each day will help his digestion.

Grooming

There are two kinds of grooming. They are brushing to remove mud and make the pony look tidy; and deep grooming which cleans and massages the skin and helps to keep your pony fit and healthy. If your pony lives at grass, use only a dandy brush, or you will remove the waterproof grease from his coat. Pick out his feet before you ride. If your pony is stabled, deep groom him every day after your ride. Then the pores of his skin are open and the scurf loose.

Speak quietly, then run your hand down the leg from shoulder to fetlock and pick up the foot. Use the hoof pick from heel to toe to get anything that is lodged there.

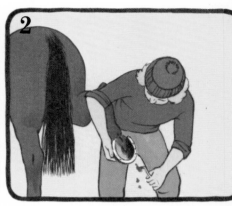

Slide your hand down the back of the lower leg and lift the hind foot in the same way. Clean out the foot like this, taking care not to hurt the sensitive frog.

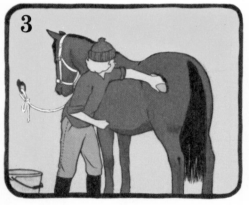

Brush off mud and sweat stains with a dandy brush. This has hard bristles and will also bring scurf to the surface. Use short, firm strokes except in tender parts.

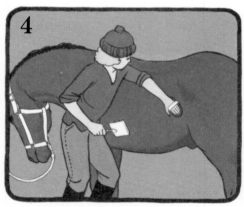

Deep groom with a body brush, using short circular strokes with your weight behind the brush. Clean the brush with the curry comb after every few strokes.

Carefully wipe round his eyes and nostrils with a damp sponge, or cotton wool which you throw awa Clean under his tail using another sponge kept just for this job.

Put the mane on the wrong side, then brush it back into place, a few hairs at a time. Brush the tail like this, with a body brush. Take care not to break any hairs.

Put a coat of hoof oil on the hoof wall. Put it also on the sole and frog if you have washed and dried them. This looks good and helps to stop them cracking.

Use a damp water brush to lay the mane and untidy hairs at the top of the tail. Lastly, wipe your pony all over with a clean cloth so his coat is smooth and shiny.

Health

Most ponies are tough. If you take good care and feed them sensibly, they will probably be healthy. But illness and accidents can happen, so learn what to look for and when to call the vet. A healthy pony has a shiny coat, bright eyes and eats well. Look out for signs of lameness, poor appetite or a dull coat. Notice if he is losing weight or putting on too much. Start your own First Aid kit with cotton wool, wound powder, antiseptic ointment and bandages.

Coughs and Colds

If your pony starts coughing, keep him alone so he does not infect others. Send for the vet. Colds last about 10 days, but your pony must be rested for several weeks.

Keep him warm and offer tasty food, such as warm damp mashes with glycerine, honey or treacle to soothe his throat. Cut out hard food. Rest a pony with a cough.

Colic

This is a tummy pain and is sometimes due to bad feeding. It may be very serious. Call the vet immediately and keep your pony warm and moving until he comes.

Laminitis

Ponies which eat too rich grass sometimes suffer from this. Tender parts in the front feet swell and become so sore it hurts them to walk. Call the vet.

Worms

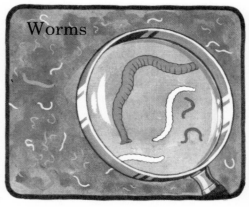

Different kinds of worms can live inside your pony, eat his food and get into his bloodstream. They will make him thin and unhealthy if he is not treated regularly.

Cuts

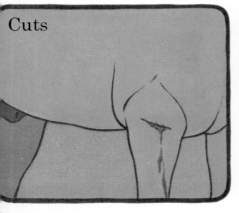

Bathe small cuts in mild antiseptic and warm water. Dry the cut and put on wound powder. Deep cuts may need stitching by the vet and the pony kept in and rested.

Ringworm

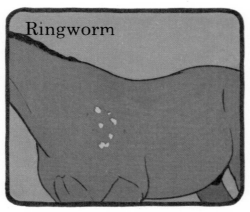

Small, round, bare patches appear anywhere on the body. It is very catching, so isolate him and handle in rubber gloves. Ask your vet for something to help clear it up.

Cracked Heels

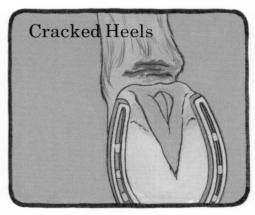

Wet pastures or too much washing can give your pony sore heels. Try to keep them clean and dry, and ask your vet for a suitable healing cream.

At the Blacksmith

Horses which run wild do not need shoes. Their hooves wear down naturally. But horses which work or travel on hard roads need their feet protected by metal shoes. The hard outside of the horse's hoof grows about 5 mm each month. This needs to be trimmed or the horse may go lame.
To do this, the blacksmith takes off the old shoe, cuts off the extra growth, and fits a new shoe.

An electric fan behind the forge blows air into the fire to make it hotter.

The blacksmith cuts long pieces of fullered iron into short lengths to make horseshoes.

Water to cool hot horseshoes.

Blacksmiths wear leather aprons to protect their clothes from wear and sparks.

This blacksmith is hammering a red hot shoe into shape.

1 Shoeing a Horse

First the blacksmith uses the sharp edge of a buffer to loosen the nails which are holding the old shoe on to the horse's hoof.

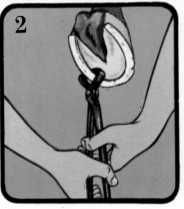

2

Then he levers off the old shoe with pincers, taking care not to twist it sideways or damage the outside wall of the hoof.

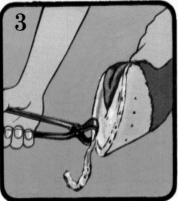

3

He uses clippers, called hoof parers, to cut away the extra wall which has grown since the last time the horse was shod.

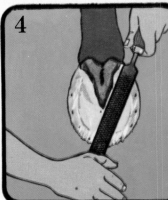

4

To make quite sure that both sides are level and that the new shoe will fit comfortably, the blacksmith rasps the hoo

Being a blacksmith is a very difficult job to learn. Young men, called apprentices, train for many years before they are good enough to make and fit horseshoes on their own.

This blacksmith is holding a horse's hind leg and rasping the hoof.

Parts of a Horse's Hoof

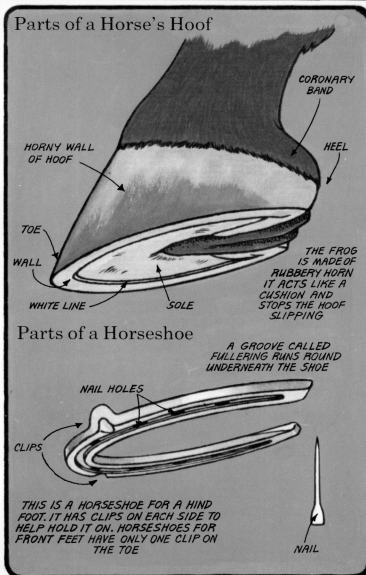

CORONARY BAND

HORNY WALL OF HOOF

HEEL

TOE

WALL

WHITE LINE

SOLE

THE FROG IS MADE OF RUBBERY HORN IT ACTS LIKE A CUSHION AND STOPS THE HOOF SLIPPING

Parts of a Horseshoe

A GROOVE CALLED FULLERING RUNS ROUND UNDERNEATH THE SHOE

NAIL HOLES

CLIPS

THIS IS A HORSESHOE FOR A HIND FOOT. IT HAS CLIPS ON EACH SIDE TO HELP HOLD IT ON. HORSESHOES FOR FRONT FEET HAVE ONLY ONE CLIP ON THE TOE

NAIL

5

He presses the hot shoe on to the hoof to make sure it fits exactly. The wall of the hoof has no feeling so it does not hurt.

6

Now the blacksmith nails on the new shoe so that the points of the nails stick out about 3 cm up the wall of the hoof.

7

When the points of the nails have been twisted off, he hammers them from underneath, holding pincers under the ends.

8
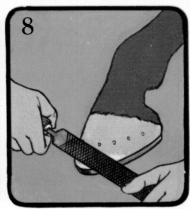
Finally he rasps the outside of the hoof and the points of the nails, called clenches, so there are no sharp edges.

In the Saddle

Always remember to wear a hard hat whenever you go riding. Before you mount your pony, make sure that the girth is tight enough or your saddle may slip round. Try to sit with your knees and thighs close against the saddle, ready to grip and keep you steady. Once you learn to do this, you will not be tempted to use the reins to keep your balance.

YOUR BACK SHOULD BE STRAIGHT BUT NOT STIFF.

KEEP YOUR SHOULDERS WELL BACK AND YOUR ELBOWS CLOSE TO YOUR SIDES

SIT IN THE MIDDLE OF THE LOWEST PART OF THE SADDLE

KEEP YOUR HE AND LOOK STR AHEAD

KEEP YOUR HANDS JUST ABOVE THE WITHERS

YOUR KNEES AND ANKLES ACT LIKE SPRINGS. TRY TO KEEP THEM SUPPLE

REST THE BALL OF YOUR FOOT ON THE STIRRUP

KEEP YOUR HEELS DOWN

Tightening Your Girth

Move your leg forward and lift the saddle flap. Pull up the straps one at a time, pushing the spike of the buckle into the higher hole.

Mounting

1

Stand beside your pony's near shoulder, facing his tail. Hold the reins in your left hand with a handful of mane, like this. Hold the stirrup with the other hand and put the ball of your left foot into the stirrup iron.

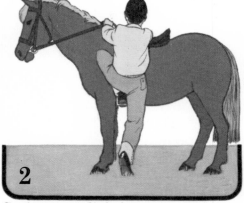

2

Spring up as lightly as possible, taking care not to jab your pony's side with your left foot. Hold either the front or back of the saddle with your right hand.

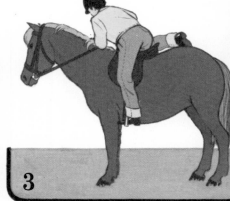

3

As you straighten your left knee, swing your right leg up off the ground and clear over your pony's rump. Take care not to touch him with your foot on the way over.

16

HOLD THE REINS SO YOU MAKE A STRAIGHT LINE FROM YOUR ELBOWS TO THE BIT

Holding the Reins

Holding the Reins

Your hands are the most important link between you and your pony. Hold the reins lightly so you can just feel your pony's mouth. From the bit, the reins should pass between your third and little fingers, across the palms of your hands and be held between your thumbs and first fingers.

Keep your hands level, one on each side of your pony's neck about 10 cms apart. Hold the reins with your knuckles facing the front and your thumbs on top like this.

Adjusting Your Stirrups

Dismounting

1

2

ll up the loose end of the stirrup ather, holding one finger on the ike of the buckle. Now you can ove the leather up or down thout losing the end.

Take both feet out of the stirrups so your legs are hanging free. Now lean slightly forward and, still holding the reins, rest your left hand on the pony's mane.

With your right hand on the front of the saddle, lean slightly forward. Then swing your right leg backwards and clear over your pony's loins.

4

3

4

t down gently into the saddle so u do not hurt or frighten your ny. Put your right foot into the irrup iron and take up the reins both hands.

Slide gently down, well away from your pony's front legs. Remember it is dangerous to dismount by swinging your right leg forward over your pony's neck.

Run up the stirrup irons and take the reins over your pony's head. To lead, hold the end of the reins in your left hand and both reins close to the bit with your right.

Paces

Ponies have four paces—walk, trot, canter and gallop. Learn to ride them correctly, then you and your pony will be comfortable and will work happily together.

Walking

The walk is the easiest pace because it is calm and steady. You have time to think about the right way to ride. It may feel quite strange at first, but the secret is to relax just enough to feel the rhythm of your pony's stride. Hold on to the saddle or mane until you feel safe, then take the reins. These are to control and guide your pony, not to hold you on.

As your pony walks, his head moves up and down. Hold the reins very lightly so that your hands can follow his rhythm. Sit well down in the saddle and try not to lean forward or look down.

The walk has four hoof beats. Each hoof strikes the ground separately in turn like this—near fore, off hind, off fore, near hind.

How a Pony Walks

Trotting

Trotting is more bouncy and may feel uncomfortable until you learn to rise. Do not try trotting until you have learned to walk. You can either sit down to trot or rise up and down in the saddle, in time with the pony's movements.

Rising to the trot is easy once you get it right. Let the bounce of your pony's stride push you up and forward a little from your knees. Then sit back gently into the saddle in a regular rhythm. Try to keep your hands and lower legs quite still. All this takes a lot of practice. It may help to say "Up-down" in time with your pony's stride at first. Lean slightly forward so you do not lose your balance. Keep your back straight but not stiff.

Your pony's legs move in pairs. The near fore leg and off hind leg together, then the off fore leg and near hind leg together. These are called diagonals.

How a Pony Trots

18

Cantering

Cantering is exciting and is the favourite pace for most riders. Remember, though, it is quite tiring, so practise for only a short time at first.

To begin with, hold the saddle with one hand. Sit up straight and allow your hips to go with the movement of the pony, so your seat stays in the saddle. You will be stiff at first and find it hard not to bounce up and down. Your hands must hold the reins so your pony's head can swing up and down with the stride.

A pony can canter with either fore leg leading. When cantering in a circle, the inside leg should lead, then he will be properly balanced. The canter has three hoof beats. When the off fore leg leads, as in the picture, the hoof beats are near hind, then off hind and near fore together, and then off fore.

How a Pony Canters

Galloping

The gallop is the fastest and most exciting pace. You should gallop only if your pony is fit and you can control him when cantering.

Ponies increase their speed from canter to gallop by taking longer strides. They push harder with their hind legs and stretch out their body, neck and head. Each foot is on the ground for a shorter time, and there is a moment when all four feet are off the ground at once.

Take your weight forward and right out of the saddle to give your pony's back the freedom to make the extra effort. Have your weight on your knees and feet. Never gallop where there are people walking or where you might lose control of your pony.

As in the canter, your pony's inside leg should lead if you are on a bend. The gallop has four hoof beats. When the off fore leg leads, the hoof beats are—near hind, off hind, near fore, off fore.

How a Pony Gallops

Aids

Every well-trained pony has been taught to understand a special set of signals from its rider. These signals are called aids. You must learn them so you can tell your pony what to do. Signals using your voice, hands, legs and body are called natural aids. Whips and spurs are artificial aids. You need quite a lot of practice to use these aids correctly. It is important that you learn on a trained pony which understands and obeys. Then you get the feel of doing things right.

Voice

Talk quietly but firmly. Your pony will learn to understand your tone and become confident, as long as you treat him well. Always keep your commands very simple. He will understand the sound of words such as "Walk" and "Trot" and "Whoa" but not long sentences.

Hands

Your hands help to control and guide your pony. Use your fingers to send messages along the reins telling him what to do. Never use the reins to hold you on. Try not to pull at your pony with the reins. This will make his mouth hard and he will soon begin to pay no attention when you tell him what to do.

Body

You can change the balance of your pony by moving your body slightly. If you change the pressure of your seat on the saddle, he will soon learn to understand what you are telling him to do. The exercises at the bottom of the page and lots of practice on the lunge will help you to control your movements.

Legs

Use the lower part of your legs to tell your pony when to go faster. Squeeze against his sides just behind the girth, using different amounts of pressure. You control his hindquarters by squeezing further back behind the girth. This helps to tell him when to move sideways or turn.

Exercises

It may seem difficult and tiring at first to ride the right way. This is because you are using muscles which do not often have to work. Try these exercises to help make you supple and fit. They are all great fun and will help to improve your riding. Practise for only a few minutes on a quiet pony somewhere safe, or with someone to hold your pony steady. Tie a knot in your reins so you do not catch your toe in them as you move about.

Rising in the Saddle

Lean slightly forward keeping your head up. Push down and raise your seat about 5 cms from the saddle. Then lower it gently. Hold your pony's mane at first if necessary.

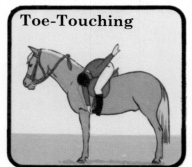

Toe-Touching

Bend down and touch your toes like this. First one side then the other. Make sure your foot does not come up to meet your hand. Do not let your other leg slip backwards.

Swinging Arms

Swing round to face one side then the other, with your arms at shoulder height. Do it in a smooth rhythm, keeping your legs quite still. Try arm circling too.

First Lessons

The girl in this picture is having a lesson on a lungeing rein. The instructor has control of the pony so she does not need to hold the reins. When you do this, you will really be able to feel your pony's movements. Hold on to the front of the saddle if you feel unsafe. A short lesson in each direction is enough, or your muscles become tired and stiff. It is important that you are lunged by someone experienced, and on a pony that goes well. Then you will be able to concentrate on keeping your balance and riding correctly.

Do not sit stiffly. Allow your body to move with the pony.

A lungeing cavesson is put on over the bridle. The rein must be at least 4.5 metres long. It has a swivel clip which is attached to a ring on the noseband.

On a left circle, the instructor holds the rein in his left hand and carries a whip in his right. His voice is usually enough to control the pony's speed.

Leaning Back

Lean forwards, from your waist. Then bend slowly backwards until you are resting on your pony's headquarters. Do not let your legs slip forward.

2

Now return slowly to the correct position. Keep your arms folded all the time. This is difficult if you are not fit. It helps to make your back and stomach muscles strong.

1 Around the World

Swing your right leg over your pony's neck so you are sitting side saddle. Next swing your left leg, then your right leg, over his back so you are side saddle on the other side.

2

Lastly, swing your left leg over his neck to get you back where you started. Do this in a gentle rhythm, taking care not to kick your pony. Then try it going the other way.

Changing Pace

Changes from one pace to another should be smooth without any jerky movement. Make each signal clear and just strong enough for your pony to understand and obey. Watch a good rider on a well-trained horse. The aids are almost invisible and this is what you should aim for. It takes lots of practice and car only be learned properly on a well-trained pony who will understand what you want it to do.

Increases of Pace

IF YOUR PONY TRIES TO MOVE BEFORE YOU GIVE THE SIGNAL, CHECK HIM BY INCREASING THE PRESSURE OF YOUR FINGERS ON THE REINS

KEEP YOUR HEAD UP

TRY NOT TO BECOME STIFF

Prepare to Walk

LET YOUR HANDS FOLLOW THE MOVEMENTS OF HIS HEAD

KEEP A CONTACT WITH HIS MOUTH

Walk On

As he sets off, lighten the contact on his mouth with your hands following the natural movement of his head. Don't lose contact completely or you will have no control.

Give a quick squeeze with the lower part of your legs and say "Walk on". As he sets off, slacken the reins so his head can move in the rhythm of hi walk. Keep sitting up straight as he moves off.

Decreases of Pace

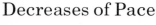

TRY TO SIT STILL THEN YOU WILL NOT UNBALANCE YOUR PONY

WHEN YOU FEEL HIM RESPOND TO YOUR SIGNAL, RELAX YOUR FINGERS

USE YOUR LEGS TO KEEP HIM MOVING STRAIGHT AND STOP HIS HIND QUARTERS SWINGING OUT

TAKE CARE NOT TO BOUNCE FORWARD AND LOSE CONTROL

Canter to Trot

Trot to Walk

Straighten your back and press down with your seat. At the same time, increase your feel on the reins and say slowly. "Trot". Keep your legs close to his sides so he comes to a smooth well-balanced trot.

As before, sit to the trot and press your seat down. Gently resist with your hands as you say "Walk".

Bring your legs agains his sides to keep him going forward as he comes into a walk.

FOR A SMOOTH CHANGE OF PACE FROM WALK TO TROT, SIT THE FIRST FEW STRIDES. START TO RISE ONCE YOUR PONY IS TROTTING IN A STEADY RHYTHM

KEEP YOUR HEELS LOW AND RISE FROM YOUR KNEES

SIT DEEP IN THE SADDLE AND PUSH WITH YOUR SEAT

"ASK" WITH THE RIGHT REIN AND GIVE FIRM PRESSURE WITH YOUR LEFT LEG BEHIND THE GIRTH

USE YOUR INSIDE LEG ON THE GIRTH TO KEEP HIM GOING FORWARD

DO EXACTLY THE OPPOSITE TO CANTER TO THE LEFT

Trot

Canter

ur pony will shorten his ck slightly as he trots, shorten the reins fore squeezing with

your legs. Drive him forward with your seat and legs. Repeat the leg pressure to keep up a steady pace.

Sit deep into the saddle. Use your inside leg on the girth to keep him going forward. Take the outside

leg back behind the girth. Squeeze with the inside rein to make him strike off on the required rein.

O NOT LET YOUR ET SLIP FORWARD. SH DOWN INTO YOUR HEELS

REMEMBER YOU ARE GIVING HIM A SIGNAL TO STOP— NOT PULLING HIM TO A STANDSTILL

SAY "BACK" AND KEEP HIM STRAIGHT WITH YOUR LEGS

TWO OR THREE STEPS ARE ENOUGH. THEN MAKE HIM WALK FORWARD

Halt

Rein Back

raighten your back and crease your feel on the ins, saying "Whoa". ress with your legs to

bring his hind legs under his body. This will bring him to halt standing square on all four legs.

This can only be done with a well-trained pony. Keep him standing straight with his attention on you.

Give light leg aids, but resist with your hands so he steps backwards instead of forwards.

23

Changing Direction

It is important to be able to ride your pony smoothly to right and left at each pace. You may find it harder to turn or circle one way than the other because he is stiff on one side. Exercises can help to make him supple.

Do not lean forward and pull him round. Sit well down in the saddle. Your seat and legs tell him what to do and your hands guide him. These pictures show how to turn right. Do exactly the opposite to turn left.

Turning to the Right

Sit up straight. Keep your seat square on the saddle or you will upset your pony's balance.

Your pony should look to the right b bending his neck, not just by turning his head to the sid

Hind feet should follow in the tracks of front feet.

How Ponies Bend their Spines

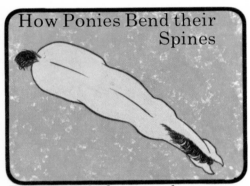

To turn or circle correctly, a pony should bend his neck and spine in the direction in which he is going. Seen from above, his body makes an arc, like this.

What Your Hands Do

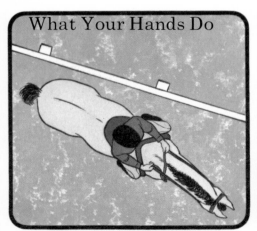

Guide your pony by increasing pressure on the right rein. Give a little with your left hand to allow for the turn. But still keep enough contact to control him.

What Your Right Leg Does

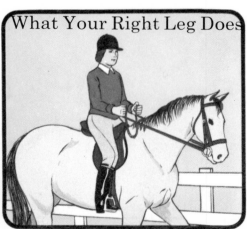

The inside leg stays in the normal place close to the girth. Your pony should seem to bend himself round this leg as he turns. Keep up a steady pace.

What Your Left Leg Does

This is the outside leg. Press it lightly against your pony's side further back than usual. This stops the hindquarters swinging out to the left.

Changing the Rein

This simply means turning and riding in another direction. Try to do it as smoothly as possible, without changing your pony's rhythm. To change from the left to right rein, follow the blue line on the menage plan below. Turn diagonally across the school at the first side marker after you have ridden along the short side of the school. When you reach the marker diagonally across the school, it is easy to change to the right rein. You can also go straight across. In a group, the leading rider makes the change.

What is a Manege?

This is any enclosed area where you can practise riding without being disturbed.

An indoor riding school is ideal, but any flat level area will do. You can use a quiet corner of a field marked off with bales of straw or oil cans. The usual size is 20 x 40 metres. Certain points round the manege are marked with letters. As these are always the same, it is a good idea to learn them by heart. Then you will know what to do without looking when given an instruction.

Exercises

Ride these exercises very thoroughly for regular short training periods. They will help to make your pony supple and improve your balance. Do them first at a walk, then a steady trot. Keep up the same speed and rhythm. It is not easy to ride circles exactly. Large ones are easier, so start with these. Imagine that a circle has been drawn on the ground. Look ahead and try to keep your pony on it. Next try a figure-of-eight, which is two circles with a change of direction in the middle. Lastly try a serpentine all the way up the school.

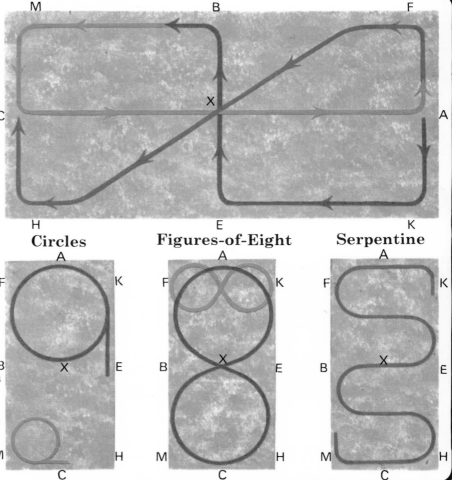

Circles **Figures-of-Eight** **Serpentine**

Learning to Jump

Jumping is great fun. But do not start until you feel secure and can control your pony at walk, trot and canter. It is a good idea to follow a plan of training, like the one below, with a teacher if possible.

Practice for short periods or your pony may get bored. Always finish when he has done something well. Have your stirrups a hole or two shorter to ride in the jumping position.

Approach

It is important to get the approach right, otherwise your pony will find it difficult to jump. Ride in the correct jumping position. Let your pony lower his head to judge the position and height of the jump

Take-Off

Make sure that you are not left behind as your pony pushes up an forward. Lean forward, but keep close to the saddle, and do not sta up in the stirrups. Move your han forward to give him plenty of rein.

Trotting Poles

This is a good way to start. It will help to improve your balance and make you more confident. Your pony will learn to adjust his stride, which is important for jumping. Use solid poles 10-15 cms in diameter and at least 3 metres long. Then your pony will really have to pick up his feet to trot over them. The second pony is following quite closely to encourage him. Once ponies know what to do, they should go one at a time.

Starting Off

Start by walking over one pole. Add more, one at a time, about 1.2 metres apart. Lean forward a little and keep a light feel on your pony's mouth.

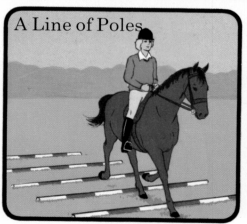

A Line of Poles

Now try at a steady rising trot. Start with one pole and then add others as before. Trot over the middle of the poles, keeping up the same rhythm all the way.

Your First Jump

When you and your pony feel safe over trotting poles, place a low cavaletto about 2.4 metres from the last pole. Trot down the line an straight over the jump.

In the Air

it still with your knees close to he saddle. Try not to let your ower legs slip backwards—then he ill not be unbalanced. He begins o reach downwards with his front egs after he has folded his hind egs to clear the jump.

Landing

His head and neck come up to balance him as he lands. His front feet hit the ground hard. You can take some of the strain off his front legs by gently moving your shoulders and seat back just a little as you land.

Away

His front feet move off into the first stride as his hind feet come down almost in their place. Take control as soon as you land. The whole jump should be a smooth, flowing rhythm. You will find this much easier on an experienced pony.

Cavaletti

he Italian cavalry first hought of these. They vanted fences they could nove easily and use to build nany different jumps. Now lmost all riders use them o train their horses. Work ver Cavaletti will develop our pony's muscles and rain him to think calmly bout jumping. You can ractice your jumping osition and get the feel of our pony's stride. Do not ollow the pony in front too losely.

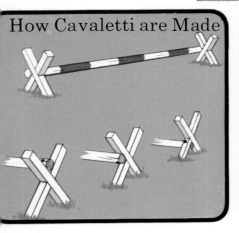

How Cavaletti are Made

You can buy Cavaletti or make your own. Make the cross-pieces with 75 cm lengths of wood 7 x 7 cm. Then fix a pole or piece of timber 3 metres long in between.

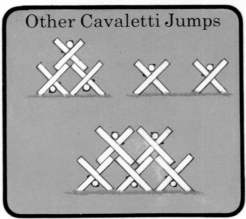

Other Cavaletti Jumps

You can make lots of different jumps with your Cavaletti. Make them low and easy to jump. Then your pony will enjoy it and not start the bad habit of refusing.

Cavaletti for Cantering

This needs quite a lot of skill. Use a pole and one Cavaletto first. Then add another about 2.8 metres away. Gradually build up a line of six jumps.

Rules for the Road

Here are some of the rules and signals you must know before riding on the road. These riders are all on the left because they live in a country, such as Australia or England, where the traffic drives on the left. If you live in a country, such as America, Germany, France, Italy or Holland, where the traffic drives on the right hand side of the road, then you must always ride on that side of the road too.

Riding on the Road

Do not ride on the road unless your pony is quiet in traffic. Keep him alert at a walk or slow trot so he will not slip or get out of control.

Turning

Signal clearly like this and in good time if you are going to turn left. Make the same signal with your right arm if you are going to turn right.

Stopping Traffic

Hold up your hand and look straight at the driver so he knows you mean him. Wait until you are sure the traffic has stopped before you cross.

I am going to stop

Wave your outside arm up and down like this from the shoulder. This tells drivers you are going to stop and asks passing traffic to slow down.

Riding in Groups

The first and last riders give signals. Ride this distance from the pony in front. Do not change pace without telling the others, or become separated from them.

"Thank You"

Thank everyone, with a nod or a smile, who is helpful. If the road is narrow and winding, go into a gateway or on to a grass verge to let traffic pass.

Riding on the Grass Verge

Ride on grass verges wherever possible, unless they are private or trimmed and mown. Never canter along a road verge. Your pony might shy into the traffic.

Leading Another Pony

Only lead another pony if you are experienced. Then have the led pony in a bridle on your inside, with his head level with your knee. This helps to control him.

Danger Ahead

Wait until the road is clear. Then ride firmly past the frightening object. Talk to your pony quietly and pat him to keep him calm. If he really plays up, get off.

Riding at Night

If possible, do not ride at night or in a fog. If you must, always wear stirrup lights which shine white in front and red behind to warn other traffic you are there.

28

Country Code

There are special unwritten rules for people who ride in the countryside. Always take extra care of other people's land and property. Remember you have a right to ride on roads, bridle paths and some other special areas. But all other fields, paths and woods are private. So always get permission first from the farmer or land owner. If you do this, behave sensibly and do no damage, you may be allowed to ride there again.

Starting Off

Check that your pony is well shod, that his tack is safe and that it fits properly. Always wear a hard hat, sensible clothes and plain shoes with a small heel. If you are going out riding alone, remember to tell someone where you are going and about how long you expect to be out.

Closing Gates

Always remember to close gates that you have opened, even if the field seems empty. Teach your pony to help you do this.

Keep to Field Edges

Avoid damaging crops and fields, especially in wet weather. Be careful not to disturb livestock as you ride through fields.

Riding Uphill

Lean forward a little to leave your pony's back and hind legs free to push on up the hill. Allow him to stretch his neck when making the extra effort.

Riding Downhill

Keep your pony steady and lean forward a little to leave his back and hind quarters free. This will help him keep his balance.

Where to Canter

Choose a quiet, slightly uphill path with soft ground, or the edge of a field if you can keep in control. Slow down to pass people on foot or other riders.

On a Long Trek

Stop for a rest of about half an hour. Have a head collar over the bridle so you can take it off to let him graze. Remove the saddle and give him a short drink.

The Last Mile

It is tempting to hurry home. But you should walk the last mile to bring your pony home cool and dry. Lead him if he is very tired or refuses to walk quietly.

Back Home

A stabled pony must be rubbed down or walked until dry. If your pony is kept at grass, turn him out and he will rub himself down by having a good roll.

Popular Breeds of Ponies

The many different breeds of ponies have special qualities of size, strength and speed, which have developed over hundreds of years. Almost all are tough, gentle and quick to learn. This makes them ideal for children to ride.

There are many different types of this popular breed. Most make good riding ponies, being tough, calm, sure-footed a quiet in traffic.

New Forest

Shetland

The smallest British breed at up to 1.1 metres. Shetland ponies can be any colour but black, brown and chestnut are the most usual. They are strong for their size and, if well trained, are specially good for small children to ride.

Pony of the Americas

This new breed was formed in 1956 by mating a Shetland stallion with an Appaloosa mare. The result was a very small Appaloosa which has become popular in America as a child's pony. Usually they have white coats, peppered with spots of coloured hair.

Fjord

Iceland

These quiet ponies are becoming more popular outside their native country of Norway. They are easy to spot by their dun colour with black legs and black hairs in their manes and tails. They make good steady ponies to ride and drive, being tough, easy to feed and very good natured.

These tough little ponies of under 13 hands were brought to Iceland in the 9th century. Some work as pack ponies. Others, which ar ridden, learn a special pace which is half-wa half-trot.

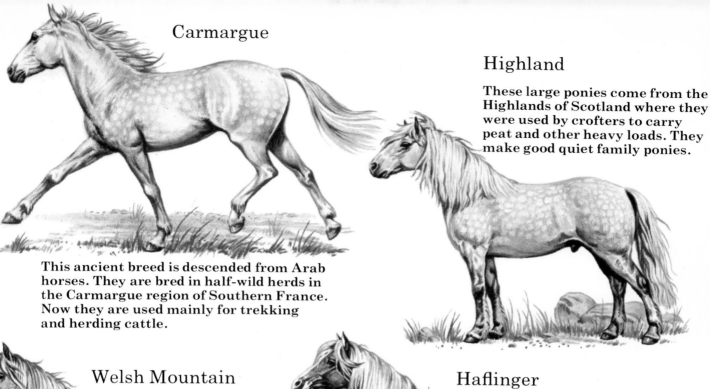

Carmargue

Highland

These large ponies come from the Highlands of Scotland where they were used by crofters to carry peat and other heavy loads. They make good quiet family ponies.

This ancient breed is descended from Arab horses. They are bred in half-wild herds in the Carmargue region of Southern France. Now they are used mainly for trekking and herding cattle.

Welsh Mountain

Haflinger

ese beautiful ponies, with flowing manes d tails, have lived in Wales since Roman es. They are popular all over the world for ing, driving and breeding, being good tured, strong and nimble.

All Haflinger ponies can be traced back to one chestnut stallion called Folie, born in Austria in 1874. They are tough, sure-footed ponies and used to living in mountains. They are now popular in many countries.

Connemara

Exmoor

is breed is thought to ve been produced by ab horses, saved m wrecks of anish Armada ships, ich bred with ponies reland. Their Arab tleness and smooth lking stride make m ideal family nies.

These ponies with light coloured muzzles still live in half-wild herds on Exmoor. They are only about 12.3 hands high, but are sure-footed, have a smooth flat trot and are fast and good at jumping.

Index

Telling a Pony's Age

This pony is under two years old. His bones are soft and he is still growing, so his rump may be higher than his withers. He is alert and interested in everything.

A mature pony of about eight years is in the prime of his life. He looks proud and confident, and is well-muscled and strong. Hollows over his eyes may begin to show.

This pony is nearly 30. He looks thin and bony. His muscles are slack and he may not eat well. The hollows over his eyes are deep and his movements have become stiff.

First published in 1978
Usborne Publishing Ltd
20 Garrick Street
London WC2E 9BJ

Published in Australia by Rigby Ltd,
Adelaide, Sydney, Melbourne,
Brisbane, Perth.

Published in Canada by
Hayes Publishing Ltd.
Burlington, Ontario.

Printed in Spain by
Printer, industria gráfica
Tuset, 19   Barcelona
D. L. B. 46470-1977